how to have fun making mobiles

By Editors of Creative

Illustrated by Nancy Inderieden

DEDICATED TO
TOM, MIKE, KRISTY and TIMMY

creative
craft
book

Library of Congress Number: 73-18210
ISBN: 0-87191-293-7

Published by Creative Education, Mankato, Minnesota 56001. Distributed by Childrens Press, 1224 West Van Buren Street, Chicago, Illinois 60607

Library of Congress Cataloging in Publication Data
Creative Educational Society, Mankato, MN
    How to have fun making mobiles.
                    (Creative craft books)
    SUMMARY: Gives instructions for creating simple mobiles using such materials as paper, cardboard, sticks, styrofoam, wood, clay and wire.
    1. Mobiles (Sculpture) — Juvenile literature.
(1. Mobiles [Sculpture])   I. Title
TT910.C7 1973   731'.55   73-18210
ISBN 0-87191-293-7

1996411

ABOUT MOBILES

Many of our crafts have been passed down from ancient times. Mobiles are an exception. The first mobile was exhibited in 1932.

An American sculptor, Alexander Calder, is given credit for making the first mobiles. Before Calder's mobiles, other sculptors had made sculptures that moved by using clock works or motors. Calder's sculptures were made of sheet metal shapes and wires. They would move when pushed by air. An artist, Marcel Duchamp, named Calder's sculptures "mobiles".

Calder's mobiles are usually made of thin sheet metal shapes that suggest swimming fish or leaves blowing on a tree. He uses rods and curved wires to connect the metal shapes and form a series. They are all hung from one point. Calder's mobiles are balanced so perfectly that they will move in even a very light breeze.

Calder's mobiles immediately attracted attention. People all over the world began making mobiles. They were even sold as toys as very small children were attracted by the movement and color of mobiles.

Today mobiles are very popular decorations. They can be found hanging from the ceilings of super-markets, shops, public buildings, and homes. They are enjoyed by people of all ages.

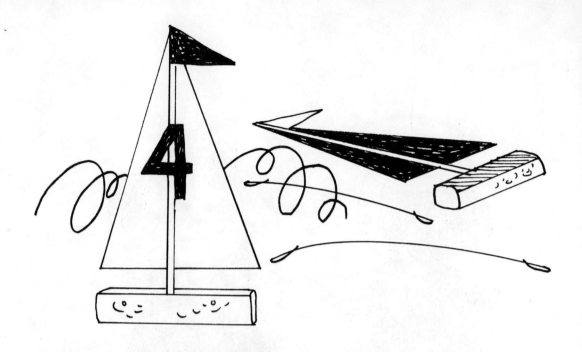

LET'S BEGIN

Mobiles are very easy to make. You do not need a lot of supplies. The most important supplies are your imagination and patience. Mobiles are also fun to make. There are no rules to follow when making mobiles. They do not have to be made to look like any other mobile. You can make them just the way you want.

Your only concern when making the mobile is the movement. This is more important than the subject of your mobile. It should move easily by a small breeze, like opening and shutting a door, or if you touch it lightly. In order to move easily, it will have to be balanced perfectly. It will be easier for you to balance your mobile if you work on it while it is hanging.

Begin by planning your mobile. Your mobile can be serious or it can be fun. You can make it around one subject and tell a story. Or you can just balance it in an unusual way. Your mobile can be made with objects that are familiar or they can be just shapes. You can have one large object and several small ones or they can all be the same size. Remember when selecting objects that there are no rules and no limits. Use your own imagination and make it fun.

Begin with very simple objects. You can make very simple ones from paper or cardboard. Or you can find some objects that are already made. You will have more fun if you do make your own objects. Copper wire or pipe cleaners can easily be shaped into birds and fish. Then you can leave these as they are or cover the insides with foil, or wrapping paper.

Once you know what subject you want to make your mobile around, gather all of the items you will need for your mobile.

If you are going to make a hanging mobile, start by hanging your string or wire. This can be attached to the ceiling or the bottom of a light fixture. Remember when attaching the string that later you will probably want to cut some off. You don't want your mobile to hang too low, so that someone will walk into it. You do want it low enough for you to work on now without standing on a chair.

Now you are ready to tie a stick or a piece of stiff wire to the bottom of the string for your frame. Balance this piece. Then you are ready to hang the objects and add other sticks.

13

The objects will be easy to attach to your frame. You will need a thread, a string or a thin piece of wire. Choose something that is heavy enough to hold your object. Balance each object as you attach your string to the object. You might even need more than one piece of string or wire to balance your object. Then balance this when attaching it to the frame of your mobile. If you don't want the string to show, use a nylon thread or an extra-thin piece of wire.

Once you have added all of your objects you will be ready to hang your mobile permanently. Some mobiles might need more than one string in order to keep them in balance. Try arranging your strings in different places and see what happens. Be sure that your mobile is not too low.

16

HANGING MOBILES
Paper Mobiles

Begin with this very simple paper mobile. You will need a piece of cardboard or construction paper that is about 2 inches wide and 24 inches long.

Glue the ends together to form a circle. Use light string or thread to hang this mobile. You will need four pieces of string to hang this mobile so that it will balance. Whatever subject you decide to make this mobile around remember that your objects should not be too heavy. Use thread or light string to hang the objects. Be careful or you will tear them with the string or thread. If you make your objects out of construction paper you won't have to worry about them being too heavy.

This mobile is perfect to use for holiday subjects. You can easily change the objects each month, if you want. Or, make a merry-go-round mobile.

Another paper mobile can be made by cutting different shapes and hanging them on one string. Each object on the string will move by itself.

Straw Mobiles

Paper straws are very easy to work with. You can bend them into many interesting shapes, and you can paint them.

First, put one straw inside another. To do this you must make the end of one straw pointed. Put the pointed end inside another straw. Turn until the straws are tightly joined. Continue doing this until you have a long line of straws.

Now, bend your straws into a shape. Hang your mobile using thread or light string. Remember to balance the mobile frame itself when hanging it.

You can now add your objects. Remember that the straws will not hold objects that are too heavy.

The objects on this very simple mobile were made from gift wrapping paper and straws. Two squares that were alike were cut from the wrapping paper. They were then glued together around a straw and hung from the mobile with string. Have fun making your own original mobiles from straws.

23

Other Hanging Mobiles

You can use sticks or wires to make other hanging mobiles.

Make a mobile by using sticks from the back yard. Use rocks for your objects. Rocks are fun to paint and would be a fun mobile in your room. Use string to hang the rocks.

Some wire is very easy to bend. If mom has an extra clothes hanger she might let you use one for a mobile. It can even be a mobile without cutting the top off. If you do cut the top off, be sure to have mom or dad help you. This is not a job for you because it is easy to hurt yourself. The wire can be cut into many pieces or you can bend it into one shape.

1996411

You can also use other pieces of wire. You might even be able to find other supplies around the house that would work for the frames on your mobiles. Try a ruler. Have fun thinking up new subjects. Mobiles are a fun rainy-day project.

MOBILES
ON STANDS

The base of your standing mobiles can be made from many things. A few suggestions are clay, styrofoam, cork, and wood.

After you have your base, you will need a piece of wire or wood to hang your objects from. Don't use anything that is too heavy. If you do, your base will tip over.

Now you are ready to add your objects. Never try to hang objects on your mobile that will be too heavy. They will also tip it over. Standing mobiles are fun when you put a flower on your base and have butterflies as the objects on your mobile.

27

CLAY BASES

To make a mobile base from clay use regular modeling clay. Flatten the bottom. Stick your wire rod into the center. You might have to bend the bottom of the wire in order to balance it in the clay.

Now have fun thinking of new ways to arrange your objects. Use paper clips or small pieces of wire or wood for other rods. Or, make one with circles from paper or straws.

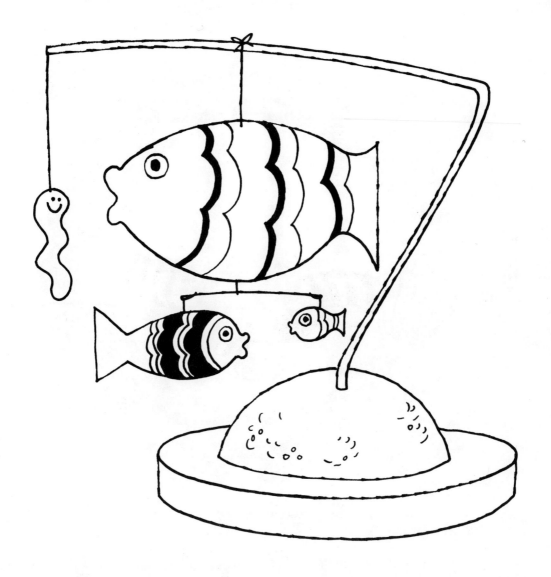

STYROFOAM BASES

Cut a large styrofoam ball in half. Glue this on a piece of wood. The styrofoam is too light to hold your frame down unless you do this. Use wire or wood for the frame of the mobile. Add your objects. Paint your base.

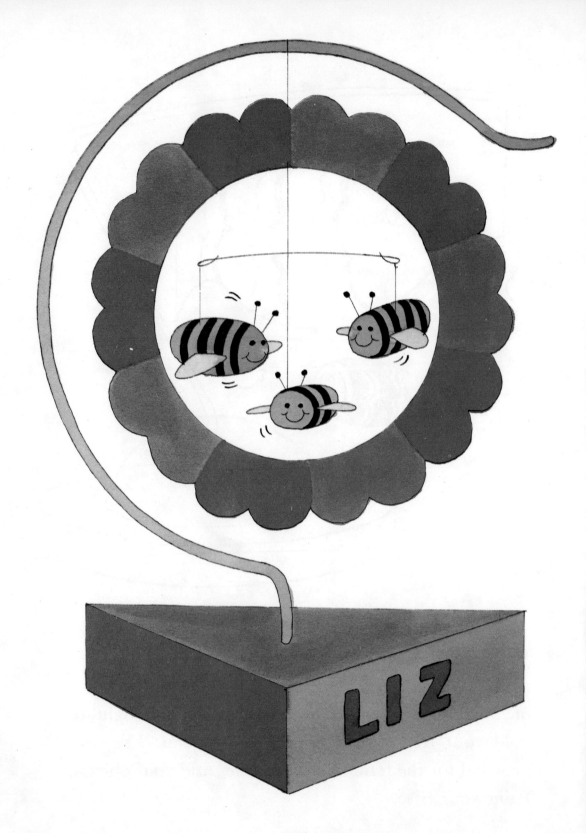

A WOODEN BASE

Have your dad cut a block of wood in a fun shape—a circle or a triangle. Then have him drill a very small hole for you to put your wire frame in. Glue the frame into place.

When the frame is set, add your objects. Paint your base.

Now that you have some ideas for making mobiles, create your own. Use your own imagination. Make a creature mobile. Or a mobile of all the planets. Have fun.

how to have fun

creative craft books